Barnyard Buddies

In the Horse Stall

by Patricia M. Stockland
illustrated by Todd Ouren

Special thanks to content consultant:
Roger Stockland, Farmer/Rancher
B.S. Agricultural Engineering, South Dakota State University

Published by Magic Wagon, a division of the ABDO Publishing
Group, 8000 West 78th Street, Edina, Minnesota 55439.

Printed in the United States.

Text by Patricia M. Stockland
Illustrations by Todd Ouren
Edited by Jill Sherman
Interior layout and design by Todd Ouren
Cover design by Todd Ouren

Library of Congress Cataloging-in-Publication Data
Stockland, Patricia M.
In the horse stall / Patricia M. Stockland ; illustrated by Todd Ouren ; content
consultant , Roger Stockland.
        p.cm.— (Barnyard buddies)
Includes index.
ISBN 978-1-60270-024-6
1. Horses—Juvenile literature. I. Ouren, Todd. II. Stockland, Roger. III. Title. IV. Series.
SF302.S75 2008
636.1—dc22
                                        2007004690

A mother horse whinnies in the warm barn.
Her baby calls back. **Neigh, neigh.**

The foal has just been born.

A foal is a baby horse. A female foal
is called a filly. A male is a colt.

The colt stands on shaky legs. The young horse is covered in soft, brown hair.

Foals can stand and walk about
one hour after they are born.

The colt shakes his short tail. He nuzzles his mother for milk.

For the first few months of his life, the colt will drink milk.

The horses are ready to leave the barn.
The colt follows his mother to the pasture.
The green grass is ripe for grazing.

Grazing is how horses eat from fields and pastures.

The colt bucks and plays in the pasture.
As the young horse grows, he learns
to graze for grass with his mother.

Farmers also feed horses hay, oats, and treats such as carrots, apples, and sugar.

The farmer starts training the colt as soon as he is weaned. The young horse will one day help the farmer herd cattle.

A horse has been weaned when it no longer drinks milk.

13

Training a horse takes lots of practice. The farmer teaches the young horse to follow commands and wear a saddle.

Horses are raised for riding, for pulling
wagons and carts, and as pets.

When the horse is almost two years old, he is big and strong enough to carry a rider.

A one-year-old horse is called a yearling. Some yearlings can carry light riders.

The horse helps the farmer herd cattle. Turning and trotting, the horse steers the cattle toward the barn.

Horses can move at different speeds: walk, trot, canter, and gallop.

19

Today's work is done. The farmer brushes the horse and feeds him oats. Tomorrow will be another busy day on the farm.

Neigh, neigh.

Horse Diagram

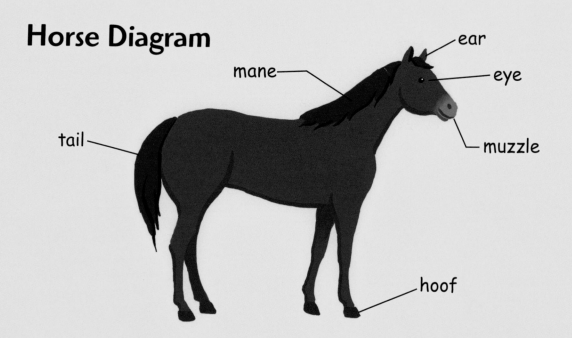

Glossary

buck—to jump.

canter—a slower type of running.

cattle—cows, bulls, and calves.

commands—directions.

gallop—a very fast run.

nuzzle—to rub something with your nose.

saddle—a leather seat put on a horse; where the rider sits.

train—to practice something a lot.

trot—a fast walk.

whinny—the soft sound a horse makes.

Fun Facts

 An adult male horse is called a stallion. An adult female horse is called a mare.

 The hard part of a horse's foot is called a hoof.

 A horse's tail is not long at birth. It takes about two years for the tail to reach full length.

 There are many types of horses, called breeds. Some breeds are big, for pulling heavy loads. Some breeds are fast, for racing. Some breeds are good at herding animals.

 Not all horses are brown. Some are white, and others have spots.

 Some horses can gallop faster than 50 miles per hour (80 km/h).

 Horses lose their baby teeth and get adult teeth, just like humans.

 There are many popular sports for horses, including showing, jumping, and racing. Horses are also used in hunting and in rodeos.

Index